Parkway

Parkway

(Hammertown, Book 3)

PETER CULLEY

VANCOUVER   NEW STAR BOOKS   2013

NEW STAR BOOKS LTD.
107 – 3477 Commercial Street
Vancouver, BC V5N 4E8   CANADA

1517 – 1574 Gulf Road
Point Roberts, WA 98281   USA

www.NewStarBooks.com
info@NewStarBooks.com

Copyright Peter Culley 2013. All rights reserved. No part of this work may be reproduced, stored in a retrieval system or transmitted, in any form or by any means, without the prior written consent of the publisher or a licence from the Canadian Copyright Licensing Agency (Access Copyright).

The publisher acknowledges the financial support of the Government of Canada through the Canada Council for the Arts and the Department of Canadian Heritage Canada Book Fund, and the Government of British Columbia through the British Columbia Arts Council and the Book Publishing Tax Credit.

Cataloguing information for this book is available from Library and Archives Canada, www.collectionscanada.gc.ca.

Cover design by Oliver McPartlin
Cover image: *Angelus Novus (for EF)* by Peter Culley
Printed on 100% post-consumer recycled paper.
Printed and bound in Canada by Imprimerie Gauvin, Gatineau, QC
First printing, October 2013

Contents

A Midsummer Cushion	3
The Wealth of Nations	6
Pause Button	7
Junco Partner	9
November Day	10
Parkway Trailway	12
North by Northwest	13
Pet Sounds	14
Ugy Edit	16
Ambit	18
A Letter from Hammertown to the Red Hook Public Library	20
Dog Eulogistics	22
Kraft Dinner With Privileges	24
Cruel Summer	26
A Poem for the Seattle Poets	29
Chicken Fist	30
Stravinsky Says	32
The Ballad of the Man in the White Castle	34
The Corner	36
The Ballad of the Man in the White Spot	37
The Ballad of the Man in the White Lunch	38
The Falconer's Tonearm	39
A Letter from Hammertown to Robert Dunsmuir	40
Five North Vancouver Trees	43
Sampler	49
MAX POWER for Maxine Gadd	62
The Inland Empire	68
A Letter from Hammertown	80
Morrissey's Code	82
A Letter to Hammertown	83

Thanks to the editors of *The Capilano Review*, *Open Text: Canadian Poetry in the 21st Century*, *Lemon Hound*, *Recluse* and *The Poetry Project Newsletter*, where some of these poems have been published.

After theatre
is our usual time for relaxation,

and following dinner
I roamed restlessly

through the beautiful
park there.

At dawn the birds awakened,
and out of their lovely chirpings

one short strain stood out.
I went back to the hotel,

and by ten o'clock that morning,
with the aid of some delicious

Amontillado Sherry, we had finished
Honey Hush.

— FATS WALLER

A Midsummer Cushion

for Rosie
and Miranda Lee

... and ductile dulness new meanders takes ...
— ALEXANDER POPE

Did we know
That when that came which we had said would come,
We still should be proved wrong?
— LOUIS MacNEICE

A widow's walk with an ashtray;
a "sleeping room"
in the old parlance

mauve sentences, bunched
letters widely spaced
a sixteenth up from the line

the blank top half of the notebook
a thickly penciled rubbing of the
North Shore mountains

ski lights a lozenge of
compasspoint perforations
biographically upfront

like the cello in the Dvorak concerto,
a big bee in a small jar,
a pancake eager for its syrup.

In an alley off Salsbury
a delicately staggering Villon
leaves perfect raccoon tracks in the spring snow.

The wild clump, the staggered row,
the spray, the earnest daisy solidarity.
The deferential snowdrops.

Talk of plants *escaping* a nice usage.
                    "... serried."

On the back neighbour's slope the lawn fades
three or four feet past
comfortable uprightness,

a natural couch though no one sits —
back there ants would be a problem.
& the skunk cabbage fell in love with the daffodil.

Sam, the patch of woods
where I "found" your
razor scooter is officially no more,
save for this wan mohawk of alderpoking scrub —

walked past today a grader
working over the loamy slash
like a chimp taking notes
... *a matter of hours.*

Trees to landscaping as books
to decorating; ominous clutter, obscene.
Peeps asleep inside or cooking cabbage

in the air where once I'd stood,
looking around for the "real" owner,
a shaven hedgeloafer out of Thomas Bewick

the last cheap real estate mid-Island
a chain of similarly
smoking copses, knotted

perpendicular oak meadow
crime scenes, Pepto-Bismol swamps.
Mountain Dew —

coloured spring growth
on the tree tips edible
according to Tony.

The Wealth of Nations

The sparrow — still stopping
by the porch daily
though there's two cats

and not one black sunflower seed not one
since three days after the snow melted
three months ago —
develops a taste for cat food.

When the paper bag twisted
onto his overhead bulb
began to singe
it was time to leave.

My vanity was that afterwords I could
use such knowledge to
move more easily between the worlds,
hang up my notary shingle

and wait for the offers to start rolling in;
for the re-incorporation of pirate islands,
for the re-branding of rum.

Pause Button

for Kevin Davies

My most precise set
of motor skills ever

working the pause button
tabletop Marantz

Peartree Meadows
vibing on a dime circa '82

by easing
a half-pinch

on the half-inch
right reel cinch

sped spread
past the head

then played back
slow

in a mist
of fast edits

fragments of Elvis
& other essences.

You had to keep
one wrong move open and

spool it out *wide* or it
might snap, thin orange 120 Sony

gold leaf thin, Gitanes cellophane
tossed & breath-bounced thin, looped

up off over the side &
fifty/fifty you get in with an old

tape you *didn't* want to hear
steak knife in hatband for

rewind sans
Keno pencil

Value Village parking lot
stock footage

scratched in black grit
a yellow car parked at a farm.

Junco Partner

Two juncos, giddy & drunk with display
on their last available hookup day
flew interlocking spirals down toward the ground
& with short hard strokes then pivoted up & around
to some pre-arranged & lofty space.
They did this in the dusty face
of burnt out topsoil where the
little forest leaned hard against a bare
woodboard fence not everyone could see.
By the fifth repetition their spiral was sweet —
if they'da been ravens they could've locked their feet —
until at the last moment, a foot off the yard,
they part as if pushed, not pivoting but hard
down again shift for two-point brakings in the dust.
After shaking off the landing, the bird just
missed the fence then turned toward it, lowered its head
and ran under, fast, toward the shed.
The other bird followed *bam!* both gone
they footchased each other onto the lawn
for quite a few feet before turning south
toward the old trees behind the house,
a place where they wouldn't be harassed —
an odd, rolling gait, but *fast*.

November Day

for Bernadette Mayer

A rumpled, desaturated flatness
eight degrees north of
Saskatoon circa '65
reconstituted "upstate",
train tracks Guy Fawkes
November '03,
the "Empire" from Buffalo to New York,
the same sloughs (though
what's the local word)
of my tar-chewing childhood.
Lake, sandstorm, snow,
The Flight of the Phoenix on a loop
DDT cloud behind insecticide truck,
hail, heat, a line spread of sedges and rushes.

The line shadows the Erie Canal
except when it doesn't.

A lot of abandoned farms
pressed meadows moult.
Blinds that wouldn't hide a crow.

The old Inland Empire materializes
out of the vapour, late afternoon
platinum glimmer off damp streets green spired
municipal buildings
granite texture of sponge toffee
aquaflecked dry fountain, thin line
of traffic slowing up for the crossing gate
whose ostinato dimly penetrates
thick railroad glass.

Across the square a plaid-skirted girl
stands munching from a neatly folded napkin
outside a bright tacqueria, registering
the low sun's polarised flicker as
it passes through.

Parkway Trailway

No more than I would expect you
to abide by the utopian stars & stripes
of your Marimekko pullover.

Late April enough dandelion heads
between here and Parksville
to keep the Island reeling for a year.
In three months enough blackberry sugar
to sweeten the nation's coffee three times over.
Sheep, llamas & alpacas dot the bare hillsides
through which pass articulated airships
laden with hemp, camphor and copper wiring.

Every third car on the monorail is a small library.

The old rail beds are still there, in some towns
gleaming tracks remain
under a peelable layer of asphalt.

Then a green carpet snaps
under your eyelid with a soft hook.

North by Northwest

for Bernd Heinrich

Fifteen feet over the porch
a plucky sparrow very handily
seeing off a raven
harassing the raven's tail so relentlessly
it couldn't get a good take-off motion
hence a series of short stalls which caused
it to drop for split seconds onto
the bandsaw of
the sparrow's ass-poking beak.

The sparrow grasped
an important truth about ravens —
that they're not very tough —
their aggression and rapaciousness
held in check by dithering caution,
curiosity edged with a
neurotic fear of the unfamilar.

They can be surprised
& thus confronted —
the sparrow must have rushed the
raven full on in a split second
& it couldn't dope it out
because the raven would never do that
lulled into a false sense of security
which must be when the eagles get them.

Pet Sounds

Under the window
at the moment of sleep
the filament of the weedwhacker

strums *hard* but damped
the first four tines from the kleenex
side of a giant comb organ.

A short length of stick,
gripped loose as in Drums 101,
twirls in your palm among

the matte jailhouse bars of the fence —
a bell whose resonant itch
burrows into your wrist.

The recycling box
bounces onto the lawn
from the edge of the frame

a second before the recycling truck appears,
the new one, which offsets
its slightness and drab yellow detailing

with the grin of its retro grill,
the esprit of the workers
can't disguise their fervor for

being outdoors, breaking things.
two thirds of an inch below the surface
of the rainbarrel the porchfish lengthwise

across a lozenge of light stretches

orange to a point of distortion,
wakes at those points

when the dorsal fin
breaks the surface,
or when the light is interrupted.

Ugly Edit

for Theo Parrish

The hollow double tonk —
timbre somewhere between
a Fender Rhodes and a child's
knuckle on a picture window —
of the raven overhead
evokes the tart agnosticism
of Dolphy on the '64 Village Vanguard
dates, each solo built up
from a couple of notes
like cell division only faster,
flipping like rural real estate,
vocalic, a wet knot of material
unravelling and then it's
laces and then it's a new knot,
a little tight which is good:

meanwhile Coltrane has installed
the drapes, driven you to the airport
and won't shut up.

Try taking it out of your brain.

An epidemic of scattered applause
greeted the "New Thing"
as out of the cthonic mists
of Hawthornian repression came
the men whose beards
had been struck by lightning —
wedding the iron control of Sousa
with the prophetic indignation
of John Brown they stood
beneath the pillars of the Williamsburg Bridge
blowing as if the rivets

would begin to loosen, the very hinges
of capital
buckle and hesitate.

A moment of silence
before six punters look up
from their drinks
in time to slap twice
in the direction of their wrists
before resuming a voice booming
multi-pocketed token search.

Ambit

A lonesome slow September bee
could let out of a lightbox be
(like me) and with some comfort
say "It's evening" — Friday's
cotillion of horse trailers,
logging, watertank and
oil trucks upped for the dry cold fall,
ATV's ridden by Ninja pyjamas, horses and horses
and riders, third wheel kid extensions
hinge off the back, traffic vests,
pennants, but no
working pedal for junior who —
tufts of feathery hair charming out
from under his helmet —
calmly regards his
mother's pumping flanks,
a digger arrives real early and
with great ceremony (still here at
10:04 but idle) on the back of a big trailer,
airbraking tired a
grumpy hiss, coughs
of oil smoke, dead stops then
swings grader round to
big Tex Avery jawdrop
to the ground, pivoting
on its forehead with
a breaker's spin
off the trailer
onto the dirt
with a soft flourish
snapsback, turns, wrenches
& is up the hill & over & out
but the trailer's too fast

as it rounds Scotchtown near enough
to shearout house
like an egg if the verge didn't grab it
a foot below the windows.

A Letter from Hammertown to the Red Hook Public Library

They wanted to hear "Baby Elephant Walk" with new ears.
STEPHEN KING, *Cell*

Was wrong as usual
about acupuncture Mike

turns out torques 'twixt
the wobble & the "chi"

do decrease activity
in the limbic seat of pain

no thanks to me or thee —
the MRI looked like my Compaq's

halting defrag, blue blocks
dimming like the lights of Harewood

used to in the pre-surveillance
eighties, not "dark"

like coffee or scary 45's
but coalmines, hot subocean vents

the upside of MacDiarmid's raised beach
& everything either swept off the table

in an excess of joy or clung to
like an eyeless Teddy shuffling

thru a mezzotint snowstorm,
chewing the sweet caraway seed at the heart

of its trauma —
but when the needle enters the skagarratic skin

turns out the red alpine static that says "prick"
is the easiest to placebo,

it's a centimeter in where
the boggle hangs it shingle

and you wake up smiling
in the crotch of the loveliest plane tree

in the park, trunk waving
in a warm hurricane of bliss.

Dog Eulogistics

> *Few people nowadays observe their dogs to grin, and those who do take it as a charming smile, but the grin of dogs seems then to have been a part of their reputation for satire.*
> WILLIAM EMPSON,
> *'The English Dog'*

Never met a detour
it didn't like,
or that didn't have

a joke at the end of it —
rara avis strode the Rare Earth
born to wonder &

born to wander,
why trees refused pants
& cats umbrellas, why

the slave that made my T-shirt,
the slave that made my donkey chow
& the slave that melted my swiss just now

don't just walk barking
over the bodies of their symptoms
& out the door, like when

it turned out the witch's
kryptonite was water, dig —
the clever flying monkeys

thought description sufficient
& didn't even have a plan A
thus found themselves a plant-mister away

from domination
by the Cowardly class —
still better under house arrest

in a postal facility
than dressed in brocade
and carried in a cup.

Kraft Dinner With Privileges

It is the pastoral idea, that there is a complete copy of the human world among dogs, as among swains or clowns.
WILLIAM EMPSON,
'The English Dog'

At last the anger ascends,
like the forking branches of a Bic tattoo
or the Lochside Fleet's rampant cross of gold,

shimmering now with revolutionary impatience
as at the Hot Club, Pol Pot slides his capo
two notches up the ukelele's neck

& after shaking out the crumbs
Lenin dries his kazoo on the radiator —
those of us who confuse improvisation

with such overpreparedness
will never understand the role of menthols
in the downfall of the Romanovs —

the Scrabble hustlers of Zurich
played through the pain,
& every croque they buttered

grilled & quartered
for the class ring & cider set
was a bucket of thick sand

dredged from the harbormouth of history.
On tiny Tampere couches they slept,
pillows stuffed with discarded beards,

rode in sealed containers down the Chuckanut

& six decades later a burning rag
is shoved through a bookstore mailslot.

At last the anger ascends — the chicken cook
is tried in absentia, his instruments
scattered to the flames while at Joe's

the Shining Path smirk through
Americanos as though at the clack of the
pool balls, while Rockit on the jukebox,

the hiss of the Victoria bus, a dog's jaws
closing on a frisbee, bandana flapping proclaim
Victory! Victory! Victory!

Cruel Summer

(after Wallace Stevens)

I

He was in Nanaimo writing letters to
Marshall, every now &
then walking down to the playhouse
for a smoke. The heavy leafage
of a wet June absorbed the roar
of the highway so he sat on the damp
carpet he'd slung over the old garden
chair & picked up and put down
the book that had begun to curl
on the dusty table raising more dust.
He trades places with the cat
so that when the gravel trucks gear
down or loudly up the cat can watch it pass
& he can pretend to read.

It was almost time for *Rockford*
when the news intervened. Outside the last
bees on Planet Earth rubbed sagey
pollen on their undercarriages.
Noting this he raised his eyes from the
newscrawl to a copper Ford drifting
thru the twilit Bel-Air of the Ford
administration. This is the part of the sublime
from which we shrink: Sepulveda, Ventura
& Culver City are to him
an approximate haze as hard as calcium,
unspooling painkillers at every point
of the compass. Something shifts &
then he shifts. He apologises
to the dead space where he had been sleeping.

2

He wakes in the pollarded half-shade of a dying
walnut. The half-audible early birds tweet
ear bones press against each other
a passing satellite pings its archive.

Night had been a tree to him moving through space,
sparing him memorable dreams, something
medication never quite achieved
but if you sit there thinking it goes dim
the golfball grain comes rushing in
like water through a window. All he knows
of the moon — its interlocking t-shapes
of broom yellow fanning
oilslick tailfeather — is that it's
both outside & above, a bell held in a cup.

The pain is such a little thing to be wandering
abroad like that. He becomes aware of the
heavy air & that he's awake,
a hiss of decompression through the leaves
hanging heavy in a hoary-hanging sky
sickly after the rain hit, turning west
he hallucinates as it falls each ring of the tree.

3

He hangs hangers in a
cupboard left to right

the wind chime's
soft memory gonging

across his neck,
Chico Hamilton style —

a handswidth or two
more or less, unstrapping

the braces, snapping brasses
hinged ruler with oil, rarely looking up,

even at those shivers of bleached
green leaf piercings

where other people move
through the light more or less as he does

but rarely with that quadrant over-the-shoulder-
you-see-what-he-sees angle — no

narrating parrot or hummingbird
or offshore bee would follow so close

knowing neither right nor left
nor above nor below

bouncing around
at the end of a pineal stalk

like the third eye of realism
squinting through the low cloud.

A Poem for the Seattle Poets

Blue from Player's Plain
Pharoah & Coltrane
hopped-up hummingbirds
raging on raw honey, oysters &
barnacle-scraping soul-encounters
buzz the pre-dawn Lynnwood rain

Blue from Winslow Homer
or someone with no home to go to
he wet his finger west
& traces out the weather week
his weakest hunch a sheriff's gut
thrust out for the informer

Blue Six's "Music & Wine"
was a song we heard all the time
before the macrobiotic encounter
split the silver monitor — the crashing
symptoms came complete
with waves of "Om" on yellow gull feet

Blue moon's a passenger with no ID
& nothing solid in the dictionary
no per diem, no booking fee,
no very convincing reason to be
alone in swollen solidarity with
the puffer, the skink & the manatee

Chicken Fist

Thanks for the purple insulator, Miranda —
Prince as Darth Vader

but in a good way —
now when I go through customs

I'll have something to declare!
The whole time I thought

I was making pearls
I was just making owl pellets

but that's ok too—
the horoscope's indication

was always a fakir's trick
with its false forking Frost faking

turnpikes not taken, but neither
road to Utopia nor

slippery slope inhibit
the spiral of growth — feel it!

we just breathed in a million ferns
in the time it took for the radio

to gear up for Tuesday recorder favorites —
in the fridge there are two experimental biscuits

that the kid in Bojangles invented us last night,
one is *epic*, the other *pastoral*

one is a bowl of milk
the other is a box of legos & an X-Acto knife,

(btw it turns out those humbos
weren't fighting because we failed to re-up

their narcissistic sugar supply
— they just like to fight!)

between the biscuits a pool of icing
has been crystalising

since the ozone hit the mountain,
no ice age to retreat from here

the sugar just
stayed put!

Stravinsky Says

I

No Mozart menu chalkboard,
he wrote at the keyboard
& orchestrated as he went along.

Tea weak hot espresso strong,
for breakfast two eggs shot raw —
before he wrote music he'd learned how to draw.

"We need blotting paper, not echo chambers," he said
To illustrate the sludge-like texture of his blood,
or spend your life with rubber-daggered strangers

dragging your feet through the Mississippi mud
standing on your head in case of a flood —
rhythms just a reminder, the rhyme's the . . . THUD —

(Mondrian — *close the window. I can't bear trees!* —)
the thing itself, forked and folding in twos & threes —
hands fluttered like turtledoves above his knees

he was the calmest man I'd ever seen.
We'll make it back to Lubeck, Texas when we can —
it's the state capital of marzipan,

Bach, Buxtehude, bernstein (amber) &
Buddenbrooks, Hanseatic laughter &
wrapping each page in a coloured ribbon after.

2

Well if the pimps outnumber the pigeons
the players still outnumber the naysayers —
"living off your income" is the new encomium!

Bush baby wrinkles checking for ammo
in a dog day dawn all swathed in pink camo,
devouring a Denny's Grand Slam Supremo —

The Institute of Pederastics
announced the Heat Death of Disco
at the moment the collected works on Columbia

could be traded for less than a light quarter of bunk,
two cartons of Newport Kings or 24 Yuengling (cans)
south of DC, post-production

thrown in for free.
No libretti, no maps, no phones —
they mostly just like to leave you alone

up to your hips in the microtones
til the cuneiform fits the uniform —
ears dragged bleeding backwards through blackberries

and dark chromatic woods
varnish through which a crystal set has played
for a hundred years on every other day.

The Ballad of the Man in the White Castle

The man in the high chair
is a critter sitter of the first order
granitic tics brush mercury hair
he folds his paper over & over

He reads with pleasure that the young
can trace their liminal state
to those distant pleasant barbecues
that did not spare the great —

With unity & impunity sundered at the root
& goofballs spared not rod nor boot
the bearshit continues, deep & crisp & even,
as though the Lemon Hart contained no lemon &

Of the great & good
there once was great many,
their shuttered doors, buckled floors
& moral miscellany —

CAN I HAZ A WITNESS TUESDAY
sd Miranda the original decider as
The Man in the White Castle
peels back paper from his slider

Corrugated as the fries he stuffs
as with deranged analgesia he puffs
a Zeppelinish tabloid in his fist
& on the wall there is a list

The bus flew over the river
The bus flew over the river

Corduroy over the river
Corduroy over the river

For zombies best a Pulaski axe
(it's the standard global chopper)
& if you have to ask how much
you ain't our kind of shopper!

Rattle of Dew in a Coke cup
ice chew till you throw up
when you gonna grow up
stop pretending that you know us

Ride the bus discussion
FOR A HAMBURGER TODAY
phone in a Vernon verdict
a double rainbow off Foul Bay

With nothing but an inset map
phone voice, head shot, leather strap
slowly he peels back the wrap
slowly he peels back the wrap

The Corner

Thirty-four crocuses
per bright square yard underneath Toilet Hill

a year & ten days ago means
its *everyone* sleeping all day this Feb.

except for the sparrow/squirrel
standoff in the walnut's big fork re:

location location location
but only for about five seconds

the sparrows puffed up double
in official waistcoats

I didn't say that no but really
not much sidle-past or back-off .

in either being though not much
endless hand-shaking malice either

but they really do look like us
or else why even speculate

let alone shake hands with 'em
eat their flesh or honey

dress them in uniforms
or fight them for money

the boundary issue
is not the territory:

a pocket atlas ends all speculation
a series of pale dashes marks the Parkway —

The Ballad of the Man in the White Spot

To create a catchment for the blood
separate the lead from the egg
strain salt through the mud
sop gravy with a heel you've begged

Spring we're still inhaling ornaments
Value Village tight with easter grails & pails
pulling tinsel through our fundaments
flossing with electric eels

This biscuit tastes of creosote
it's a stratiagraphic morsel
a puck in a vice on rice is nice
for packing plaster on the torso

Work it with a bent skate key
while acknowledging long math
let's sift this stretch of crumbtray beach
as if our habits formed a path

Then it's "later..." like the kids say
trailing off on ceramic shins
over links, tussocks & hard-step curbs
using their hands as fins

The Ballad of the Man in the White Lunch

Former site of
the last lumpless oatmeal
east of the Occident

lodge toast & oleo
curled into a cone
& softened wi' tea

reach through the bars
of the nectarine crate
giant White Man dread

brushes blood from the marble
passes the HP Sauce bottle tower
spears his patty with a pin

smoked oysters toothpicked
on the Greyhound north to Terrace, thus
between the institution

& the raw end of the polisher
November of '77
threescore & ten skins got you a hot tap

a heater, a prayer blanket
of sky & all the fortune cookies
you could eat, vitamins

a cubic yard of steam inhaled
pivoting from the sprouts
in the lobby a labyrinth monochrome

Electrohome dispensing
afterschool *Dark Shadows, Funorama,
The Kissing Man, Edge of Sleep* . . .

The Falconer's Tonearm

Bound a dime with a length of twine
plowed the licorice earth with bone,
load-bearing chords dropped off the spine
in shellac'd redoubts of Fonotone.

For the sake of us feral kids —
necks scratched raw in a two-horse town —
the sleeping cops of Michigan
poured out a can of Motown.

The thistled face of Jimmy Shand
in a flat of some small size
the hypno-coin of Frankie's face
spinning steamships past Reprise.

Brown Shanachie cottage
Angel feather frottage
this too is collage
as a function of knowledge.

Woke up this morning
began with a word —
a letter of warning
concerning a Bluebird:

the weather around Fats Waller
obviates the squalor
which is more than I can say
about Dynaflex RCA.

A Letter from Hammertown to Robert Dunsmuir

I

Screw you
Scrooge McDuck,
Born near Kilmarnock,
You built Craigdarroch
but preferred a hammock

                     ... how else

given the militarization of one's home space
but to reply in kind &

tactically, to return
smug valuation with superiority

& punch for punch,
til over each great crime is grown

a grove of alder
til over each great crime

grows a shade-spreading lime
that on a brown bench curled

I can sleep beneath until
two years after 2012 when it'll have been

a century since the bunch of us
last addressed our masters thus

in tones of such insolent rue
that their empire bled black & blue &

was forced to re-colonize
in forms a voortrekker

would recognize:
towns until then

bereft of a copper's tread
now patrolled by one of meathead

Bowser's "specials"
dredged up & barged over from Vancouver

pointed Maxim guns to & fro
(to derision & innuendo)

but when you're in that corner trapped,
squared by someone else's map & no one

downhill to pass it along to anymore
& beyond that only Pasta, Saskatcha

or Chimera, Alaska
that string of smoking islands

where Vico's giants
have dug condos into the sandstone

or a street in Honolulu
named for a nurse

from where Dick the mines inspector
& Farquhar his deep-pocketed admiral

return richer via Surrey's
crosswords & curries, their ship-in-a-bottle

aesthetic still operative
among the locals today

subject to arbitrary poking,
driving hummingbirds into the house

of your head, driving out
religion & solidarity

picnics on Shell Beach
on the islands off Shell Beach.

2

Orcadian fiddle music survives
in the high arctic

the last latticed leaf
of the HBC's

imperial tree, after
& century & a half the

viking stream
reduced to a trickle

& the rigid tripartite
of the reels stretched like ragas

the better to suit
the long dances

of mid-summer,
loosening by tallow light

messages
in knotted leather.

Five North Vancouver Trees

for Lary Bremner

Here and there between the pages a skeleton leaf conjured up those lost woods
— PATRICK LEIGH FERMOR

I

The phylogeny of sleep
vs. the ontogeny of waking up

bunnybeard blankets
dewdrop the sleeping slutswool

drooled voices skitter
from the back of a tent (circus)

useless user fingers pinch
filched bodega grapes

awake in sheets so soft
you devour them in a dream

goosefeathers knuckle
a wet November no-hitter's

bloody stucco,
horseradish breezes

curl brown paint from gray lumber
in soft curls —

an August half-moon
teething at sixes & sevens,

in sheets so soft they squeezed
phantom pain out of real pain,

excuses thumbed a map's wet fold,
a ghost train fringe marked with

misty rivers, chenille fingers, flutter gulches,
cross-digging legends out of anthracite

shaded parks bunted for cornerboys
that flap & tumble & shamble.

2

All is Loch Elsewhere,
Arcadian pancake & parkade,

chewed venue, through potash
& slough

eelgrass aftertaste
past castle & ledge

where the blue bus humps
up & left, past the twinkling figurines

of a presumptive distance
even darker closer in & thickened so with

baronial fences & colonial hedges that
only from overhead can

the security corona be glimpsed
when cat-like you trip its cricket senses.

3

All is Cantaloupe Causeway
a shrubbery of near attainments

half-rendered blossoms
a spider's tincture grown over

a monkeypuzzle half-hardened with honey —
lichen overhangs the wavy cavy air

dream-flies sip hat-salt & eye-salt & sea-salt,
& in the inky truffle shade of a giant oak

plotters tip cordials, toast
Lost Illusions, lost dogs, lost wages —

a bubble is a mighty fine thing!
For about three months & change

the tulip was worth more
than the picture of the tulip!

& that tapioca backwash
wreathed in strawberry Quik

was like childhood in reverse,
open to the nourishment but still

popping the air's envelope,
brakeless on a banana cruiser.

4

The state couldn't catch a fucking cold
too cheap to keep the flow of piping hot

up just ask the bus stations
& movie theatres —

no fresh towels for popcorn paws
& foam alone won't disinfect

the coughed-on loonies & toonies
that insist into our minty mitts —

thus later asleep, drop in throat
half-lodged (eucalyptus), I missed it

when the Matrix dropped his
crystal set into the toilet tank

& so soap-bombed the Italian fountain
that the concrete fish

crested the foam all over downtown
scales glinting off the pebbles

in the giant bowl of the casino's
outdoor loser ashtray.

5

In sleep so thick
the panels of the trucks

pivot through the birds & bricks
that flap above the viaducts

on downs as soft as poplar fluff
graders scrape off mossy stuff

revealing projects never needed,
zombie gardens never weeded

& ragged couches burning fleece
prompting no visit from police —

a hermaphroditic order
in the standing water

a kind of turbid flux
flaps above the viaducts.

Sampler

*in memoriam Jonathan Williams
& Gerry Gilbert*

*The Rural Parkway — Wooded
is characterized as
the "cut through the forest"
quality created by
the regularity of the forest edge
and by the relative closeness
of the forest to the roadway.
However, where the opportunity
to separate the bikeway exists,
it should be seen
to enter the forest
not just make the right-of-way wider.*

I

Skutz Falls on
Bruckner's 4th
non-fog salvia's
anecdote the antidote.

Clarence Bend
broke then re-broke the ice-ends
confectioner's toffee holes
patched the interior.

Gravel spot-welds
baked the basket's granite
into flakes of fondant
iced with dust.

2

Fornicating leaves
of each five one's turned upward
the vestige of Fielding Road
not excepted.

Mythago Wood
screech of harrier
screech of owl
permission to dig.

Sump path empties
into high river death splash
paint can pukes
its last bridge tag.

Landfill campers stumble
four steps from the fence
mouths full of pebbles
gullets full of debt.

Enormously reduced
by reverse mapping
muskeg description
pamphlet's gutter.

3

A newly formatted
raven's tongue
pops digitally out & in

of trombone beak
Texas jug band style
but overhead no newscrawl

no basslines from inland terraces
or hoots from hominid heights,
offroad daytrippers drop

off arbutus cloudtops
badger into a crevasse
midwestern cushion full stop tree

bent under a towhee
the tread of a groundwater smeller
rumbles through the cellar.

4

Dig & tug
where it's soft
& not drained off.

South from Alaska
a *Rockford* smog bomb
digs its own tomb.

Fill's chewed up & gone over
Fill's gone off
Fill's gone fishy.

A vacant lot's
a mountainside —
to which you're tied.

Parked at an angle
parked with struts
the runoff runs through the ruts.

A softball meteor
redly sat except it
can't be brought back.

Magnetism's a tip-off,
so's the iron fillings
of the rent-a-cop.

5

No used bookstore
on the moon
no white grow-tent puff

no Atlantis
no inflation
where the pampas meets the rough

no use for the facetious
paperback feces
produced by our species

on fire when I bought it
I dropped it & fought it
just like they taught it.

6

The reasons why I mumble
are numerous
& far from simple

from truck to trestle
bare arm tickles
conjoined freckle

we talk handshake talk
Harewood muscular under the dome
or pigeon walk home alone

wooly Bouvier wrists
grasping cans of Lucky
or freezer burn slushies.

*The edges of this type
of Parkway are defined by
the "loose" or "feathered" landscape edge*

*which may include rural fencing.
In this type of Parkway
visibility into developments*

*is expected and therefore
the controls focus
on establishing*

*a relatively consistent
building setback,
controlled signage*

*and mitigating
the negative impact
of loading areas*

*and other unsightly
elements
of development.*

7

A ferry receipt's too thin
for the sort of work engaged in
by a jimmy-wielding skeleton

& the crocuses would like to know
if spring is here or will it go
the way of *Doctor Zhivago*

garden shovels in a row
outside Rona row on row
yellow blue green yellow

our reno hit a rock
our reno hit the hard pan
our reno hit a wall

a business card's too thick
for all but thin-lipped heretics
stirring their Kool-Aid with a stick.

8

No need to get
into a stewpot
with a sacrificial horse

these days of course
a streak of Bovril hot
from tartan thermos

the battle of the trees
& the battle of the letters
& the battle between the

the letters & the trees & the rocks
has got me threading
paternoster naps past dawn —

I am the falcon
I fly blind
through a progressive sky —

Hampton Hawes
Hermosa Beach his
harmonium gently weeps.

9

*Fencing should allow for feathering,
undulation and fragmentation
of the landscape edge to occur*

*so that the fence is sometimes
in front of and sometimes behind
random groupings of indigenous*

*coniferous and deciduous
plant materials.
Open views to pastoral settings should be retained.*

*There are frequent views
through
the landscape to the rural development beyond.*

*There are view
opportunities
to the valley below.*

Something
you said once
is why there's
a past tense.

Anyone
can say please
that's hurtin' —
tell it to the second person.

Vicodin country
by funicular entry
Rancho Relaxo
by appointment to the gentry.

Vestigial barb
on a red branch
plausible to pollen
but otherwise not often.

Somedays
the heat's off
& spring goes out
the open window.

Talismanic
ordinary chalices
huddled masses
take their chances.

Advancing thought
like they ought
the moon trails its coat
across their throat.

11

I wish I could sing
like Ronnie Drew
instead of sounding
just like you.

With a nickel
& a nail
the Thursday freight
his voice derailed —

foghorn from Goldfinch
to Joanna
from Elizabeth Street to Valhalla

something a circling bird
discerned
in meaty terms

what was said & not said,
a hammering on
an empty head.

Empress Citation
disturbeth not
the quails at their suppers;

though the lookout
shoots through
the sweet-pea undercoil

then squawks left six feet
for everyone else
it's just another brindle head

patrolling loose & low
along the overgrowth's
trackside pharmacopia.

MAX POWER for Maxine Gadd

UNDER BYZANTIUM
from THE SUBWAY OF THE CONFEDERACY

CALLING FOR LONG BOWS IN THE BEDLAM OF
   BUTTONS & BOWS

The map is not the territory. It isn't even the territory. (Joel
   Oppenheimer)

"Bun" is such a sad word, is it not. And "man" is not much
   better (Samuel Beckett quoted by Maxine Gadd)

CAPITALISM IS CAUSED BY WARS; COMMUNISM
   BY FLOODS

All history slides into Whig History

Yu feel at ease with yr amnesia

that is the story of us & how we became us
& how it becomes us
to so naturally occupy
our exalted place in the scheme of things,
                    at the end of things.

NO WAY TO RUN ANYTHING, PRETENDING
   THERE IS NO AUTHORITY

Even the present disposition of
la cosa nostra, post-avant-garde poetry —
a corpse from which increasing amounts
of blood paradoxically seem to flow —
disports itself as though
its shuffling zombie compromises
were the best of all possible worlds
nuked in the eighties

or that the public life of poetry is
somehow best sustained
by using higher education
Nibelungen style
to convert the enthusiasm of young people
into credentials & debt & gelt —
by mining their good will
as one would clearcut a hillside
into a smile —
into an assumed permanent natural order.
Rendering unto Caesar.

God loves only Augustus.

Byzantium lasted ten thousand years.

This contract has given all the communities of
contemporary poetry, for all their competing modes
& methods, an underlying unanimity
borne of fear.

They make you look now at
the shape of your baby rage.
They intervene in time.
Your feelings are a symptom.
The threat of poverty & prison & homelessness & murder.
They show you the tools they would torture you with.

Thus the industrial academy
not only best arbiter
of discourse but rainbow bridge
time machine transporter slippery slope
between Bohemia & the middle class,
a reversible prophylactic.
IT ALONE LAMINATES.
It is the vessel inside
which we have agreed
that the radium of poetry

is best protected from itself;
all we ask is a bedbug snuggle in the folds —

as the economic circumstances
which encourage Bohemia have faded
from possibility
so too has the memory
of their former vigour,
history being written by the owners of horses.

They make you forget that it could have gone either way.

Not so much a split then
between the campus
& the coffeehouse
      but a flower of pure heresy — a real floater
in the patriarchal bowl
embarassing & antithetical
autodidacticism self-correcting
bibles with red protestant pencils
jutting from their spines
never beloved by
the people with guns & horses. The glamour of the Romans
marched ahead of their armies. The wise Hungarian boys
wanted in.

Thus Sibylline
neighbour wrestles with starting
the collectible collective chainsaw
Texas massacree style. But for no woman is the shadow
of the Imperium ever absent or
the rumbling engines silent.

So Max for decades sans the benefits of the kind of
eccentrically overproducing
alternative steady state personality
apparatus that keeps bissett going
& sustained Gerry Gilbert for decades

Tim Lander & me for that matter
hiding behind our beards our city.
Wearing out our knees on the welcome mat
& as boys we get to do that

but we never get to say

me thinking to kill whoever speaks to me

just like a woman, not in a woman's voice when
there was still a chance heresy might bust out & take over,
the winds of Vatican II, Prague summer,
Roberts Creek. In BC you could get away from the state
by walking uphill barefoot for ten minutes
— the British Empire hates mountains
as much as the Romans did. Build a fort on
the lip on which the sun never sets
& keep those good snacks &
drugs & trade goods coming.

We congratulate ourselves for even trying
our good thoughts & a
dollar store resembles the interior of a bandit's sack.

Babies as weapons for Mother Canada.
Dog on stun.

THE HEAVY METAL DIAPER GET SET READY TO
   GO

not even feminists
have agency
without a society
to quit

So from here on in the gendered
rejection of Satan & his works
seems a pretty clear choice.

Pride the first indicated voice.
Speaker not keeper.
Ignore the thickening local ghosts.
But the beats were as scared of Peggy Lee
as everybody else. Uniformity of conduct & sweater
mad men how even as men
can we imagine it. Hippy fascism.
Waldorf Willendorf.
Postwar /////

For if yv diddled in the truly amusing the king jumps yu

Dicks working out their shit with chicks
in a very entitled fucking way.

Bail on even as much of this
life with father figure fascism
as what sugared the rim
of the rapidly organizing poetry apparatus
& you do get privileges:

One is you get to jump off the
whole whig history train,
unshackled by utopic kiwanis klub
pinko bullshit
or future shock payback
or death on the installment plan.
But the long line of heroes is not up to you
& we'll still give you up to the cops in a heartbeat
& no you can't use our library
& you're one of the greats but
there's a coffee filter burqa
I'd like to wrap around your head —

but everything still gets to happen at once
so the nineties of saddam
the sixties of mailer

& the noughts of oh say thomas fucking friedman
vs. the placebo syndrome

PERMISSIONS you out NOW
FOR prophesy

"places people can take you & put you"
writes Max in the nineties
remember? the happy ending of history
with full release? WHAT COULD THE LIARS PAY?
In the absence of assassins
In the neural networks of high-tech
shining path star-whackers —

> *mind your wants*
> *cause there's someone*
> *that wants*
> *your mind*
>   (george clinton)

less discrete weave
of shiny life
folded in twee boxes
than inconvenient stops on
the Mandelbrot skytrain,
unsurprisable ghosty
unsurpassably bubbling up
every exchange
AGITATED PRESBYTARIAN VOLCANIC
    SUBTEXT
the void of conception
residue
of a swiping hard thumb
race against metastasizing facts
otherwise
Lost to Language —

The Inland Empire

for George Stanley

I

The weak solder
of Solidarity — Zonko's
"Hang the Sock-reds!!"
in his best Queens in Victoria
under the gaze of Victoria
who looks like a young Mary Tod
or a bomb-wielding Avignon pope,
under the gaze of the rank & file
who can't wait for Jack Munro
to come out of the snow
to get them off the hook
& back to Nanaimo.

*"when the poets start
it's time to leave"*

A farewell
no less permanent
for its awkwardness
& accompanying banners.

The Island Highway
is the tinnitus
of the landscape,
fifty words for wet snow
words over wetter snow
breaking a stick
off another stick
on my breastbone
then banging
the lichen loose
a layer of something
is the thing

slurry under slush
steel toe cow catcher

but it's not the North
not the dog of the North.

2

This snowball smells like fish
& down the same railroad cut
which carries the ascending whine
& keening rumble of traffic sometimes
bacon, smokes, coffee, acetone
pigshit, cowshit, frying chicken
(if less of the burger onion
startup combo casserole
than years since)
weed, the horse-farm
goat, always the greenwood smoke
at the bottom of the bowl.

Yellowed Penguin pages
ordinary leaves of Don Allen
failing transmissions from off-island
subject to frequency modulation
& infant theft, the last
ethered sunlight of Grade 11
a slice of lemon pound cake
from which the rind
had been removed.
Morse code
from a coffin.

Idea of North
Protestant North
no California lemons
bareknuckle bonhomie
pubs heated by sweat & breath
& pickled egg farts
terrycloth tonsure
cards 'til daybreak
a winter without hugs or drugs
hockey fights & hockey kisses
the rolling greyscale

of a cheap TV
into which the test pattern
has been burned —
conditional recognition
not so much as a poet
as one *marked off*

as that injured aldermanic raven
walking bent through the snow &
toward the fence
with an entitled eye
to the point of death.

3

This snowball smells like expired aspirin
with diesel upchuck copperhead breath —
but then what?

I wish Captain Beefheart
had played more clarinet,
the terrible headaches I would get
after parties from being at
them too long, through orange streets
to the 7–11 — plume of vapour heat
in the cold Adanac back room
digitally added with optical zoom —
On Lok tap running closed tight
walking through a big stripe
across Victoria & Hastings a big red stripe
oh it's bad in this kind of thing
when the opera lady starts to sing
& it goes all sepia, an ocarina
hand a sandstone screen,
a quarter inch of pink snow
cast iron stumps where though
they'd taken railings away for the war
Dad said we still paid & paid
getting it back in the form of blades
& Starfighters, well into the decade.

4

Lend-lease. The price of peace.
People that had figured out,
ways to make money, to tout.
To spiv. Cut your hand on his
wing collar, you could.
A mustache behind, a hood
a brothel creeper, a secret weeper.
A solid ten per cent
his demob suit rent.

Thus from the stage of the Commodore
the Captain turned & said

Read Wyndham Lewis
Apes of God! Apes of God!

meaning, I guess, that even
the over-egged & overdrawn
grotesque dreadnoughts
blundering bitterly through
the baking heyday pages
of the Torquemada modernism
I'm glad I missed
are more interesting
than *you* assholes —
I'm going to go home & paint!

But the Commodore bathroom
is everywhere, they only
pretend to stamp your hand
a pot flung into your face
half-amusingly
forever — never
a good town for crowds

they just up & leave you lonely
rather than bringing
the audience home
rather than just going home.

5

It's never quite clear
what they're up to
the men who live
on wires & shelves.

A shitstorm of data
a shark that walks on land
the amount of snow won't matter
to the phone in your hand.

Mahler's 1st
Jimmy Caan crossing Roebling's bridge
in a Cadillac to deliver
leaves to the Harlem River.

Bird shadow in the big holly
lost in the dust on the shade
forced air feathered melancholy
fluffs the scratch the branch made.

The men who live on wires & shelves
are mute even to themselves.

6

Tough to do
the working class
in wide screen:
the interiors
don't quite add up,
tables bump lumpy chairs bump
bumpy walls & let's face it
this potato-textured
distressed distress
is something you
don't want to see
in letterbox HD —
not meth-breather tubing
with a regional twang,
expository dentistry
soaked in Tang —
all except maybe
the pearl of the litter
the squirrel-skinner
with secret pluck
& historical luck.

Tough to look though Joni
from both sides now
the imprinting's all frayed
the head's dragged up & round about
like busted bell bottoms in
a cube of splayed &
pawsmeared plastic
heavy on the shoulders
eyes a cellular habit
lenses chipped & bouldered
tiny fingers still working
qwerty under the awning
speech replacing gum

chews television for the eyes
metamorphic sum

like watching paint dry
or foggy molecules bead
& dance in the light
from my hat
shakes her head
on the tracks.

7

Class fenced but from the
upside only
not a compound but

an hedgerow Maginot
a pinball's tilted
bumpers to keep the lawn

from sliding downhill
to the holler's more collar-
based trenches & redoubts, big dogs

& smaller sightlines
curved streams
with salmon-bearing couches

thickets with frogs & birds &
valentine skunk cabbages,
clotheslined yard beasts wired tight

behind a grow so obvious —
perennial mossy boat & car
plastic-sheeted dowling pyramid

the Frig-O-Seal
pie container lids tied with
orange ribbon

that everyone uses
to mark off
the marked off,

tidelines of floods
both frequent &
unseasonal —

that it must be a *choice*
like lighting the torches
for the return of the DC-3's

laden with Spam & medicine
years after the storm of the century
had swept through the valley.

A Letter From Hammertown

... to the person who dumped four
green bags of garbage
behind the Edwardian aggregate slab

on a slate knob
out of which flapped
insect wing & fern fossils

a prescription for child's ear medicine
(thank you BC Med)
revealed your address:

[withheld]

but let's not go there
use the pickup
perform the perimeter slow

an August afternoon sniff
follow the crooked track
whither where it wanders

then build a fence at eye level
over which we tip
whatever blackberry shit

beneath a half-decade
of barbs chewed
with green teeth or picked

cleaner with gleaner planks,
whatever the water table
won't hold down —

fastened then driven then hid
with certain care a split lid
randomized by ravens & raccoons

flattened by rain braille rime tuned
melancholic generic cola root beer
box saw you sit & sip with your sore ear.

Morrissey's Code

for RA

Adjusted the rain
for rheostatic intervention,
to walk so far so slowly
was never my intention.

I had arrived
at Bentall station
by unknown forces
& monstrous motivations.

By the time I got out
of the octagon
the Broadway bus
had come & gone.

In the bus stop gravel
I dug a pit
into which I dropped
a cigarette.

Consonants interrupt
alluvial flow
that's where
the letters go.

Annulled immediacy,
a cloud with eye holes
a blunt expediency
dispensed in vials.

A shadow falling
on the snow
that's where
the letters go.

A Letter to Hammertown

    I

The orange chestnut canopy has shredded
into a discarded hamper
of wet umber, umber-orange,
lacy amber, blood-orange
& bloody amber rags
through which tires carve calm channels in time,
neat stripes of a general widening
as the averages catch up.

I snobbishly note on Shasta's behalf
the oddly spindly thighs
of her underemployed big city sisters
short-leashed
by fedora dad or leopard mom
insulting white bags
threaded through their collars
a badge of slavery —
no sniff, no FIELD, no flicker.

On the soundwalk the light
is louder than I remember,
darkest in the undertree gloom
dramatic gravel bony underfoot
until cranked across by cable car,
eighties rain filtering
through a carpentered forties porch
onto the basement suite stairwell.

Twin ghosts of my brother
pass each other at different times
& don't look up.
wary, preoccupied, in transit.

Later I made a loop
of the pebble crunch & engine
so that they'd course
through her headphones
& make a kind of disco
that I could then loop again
& install in a top branch
under the streetlight
a kind of permanent radio.

Missing though: the persistent
sense of misdirection, the relaxation
of muscles associated
with certain vocabularies,
the slow rounding off
of matter under successive waves
of daylight & water.

The next day the microphone
was a hummingbird
extracting sugar from ink,
hovering locked sentences
breaking up in a
riot of orange lichen
& red bricks flattened under solar flares.

2

I abandon my self
to a blushing
of precise boundaries,
like where a squirrel would
step up to snap the branch
back fast enough
to ride the torque all the way back,
a walnut under each arm —
getaway with intent to spring
rather than English leave.

It's why I wear my
shirts backwards
& my jacket is the color
of the sky.

I'd abandon everything
for a plush spring
with a fat calendar,
every day ringing a bell
every day floating
in a penumbra of sound
echolocalic lenses unfurling
coiled batwings flap
as I velociraptor
among rainy streets & thread
on a knotted length of fishing line
pinpricks of orange brick
mixed with holiday sweat.

You abandon yourself
to the runnels & channels
of a new boundary,
ankle-deep sliding
thick transparency mirroring
even when disrupted

the thick marine light
located by inference
the waggle of a last leaf &
two minutes of leaping edit
is a spray of divided attention,
your lupine shoulder dropping
hot science on cold water.

3

The truckers eat on the roof
& the roofers eat in their trucks
tossing wax paper
out the window
until a cleansing thermal draft
sweeps the top of a cherry-picker,
a microbranded
cyclist smoking a Drum blunt
squishes in half-sleep his thigh
pyjama dancing headset tuned
to the sound of a fan
or a tiny big band
but never opens his eyes not once —
an infant navigator
in a chrome helmet
racing the wax paper.

At the highest branch
of the chestnut an FM transciever
relays sounds from the street
to another in an alder
on the shores of Beck Lake
the chestnut is only discernible from the attic
on very quiet nights during frog
season or during storms
but the one on Beck Lake carries traffic
sounds at all times over the reeds,
only fading at the forest canopy.

4

& in sleep
the furious forest
reconstitutes itself
the ringing silence
thick fleshly endrenched
footfall & Shasta's fast footfall
lakeside endorsement
underalder endorsement
ringing antennae of sleep
along the long hillsides
always stumbling & climbing
gravity heavy feet prescient sleep
sleep coming to each limb
separately heaving
the will forward fall asleep
walk & fall asleep
along the long lakesides.

Run & drift awake
the stubble of vocabulary
swirls around your feet
in spouts of antique bliss
the furious forest
now suffused with a pink x-ray light
under which the bones
of the street are revealed in
arched & baroque forms
ringing byzantine brass
through coloratura speakers
interrupts the operations of sleep
along the long avenues
always always climbing
the will forward will fall asleep
& run & drift awake
along the long lakesides.

5

Doesn't everyone need a stapler
to bind with fallen leaves
their lists of unassailable demands?

A scotchtape splice
to return dead voices
to the brink of audibility?

A stubborn hippie structure
a bottom-heavy grid
a moving sidewalk portrait?

On the second soundwalk
the streetcorners bulged
with cartoon furniture
& clouds of silent winter gnats
swirled around the ducts & fans
I'd closed my eyes against
the expected unexpected birds
who kicked the waterjug downwind
stuck firecrackers in the gravel
held electric toothbrushes
against lampposts
the expected unexpected
tricolor of bad country fireworks
strobing raccoon morse code
through the left-open gate.

Better though to lay down on the curb
ears pressed hard against it
like GC used to
to catch those long lonely city tones,
through the headlamp glow
instructions were just
ghosts in purple offices anyhow.

*Klondike? Do you hear what he
called me? Aren't you
going to fight him?*
Put together drunk, grinning
at her *favourite brown thing*
who's mock-desperately dialing a cab
on the unmanned cash machine
her filled-in diastema
sinking through cookie
to cold whiteness
The other ones are called gaps . . .

An interval then
diastem
as you step through
this rip of surface tension
into another world —

& just as my father
carried a pint for his father
home from the pub
covering it with his hands
from the rain
I will carry this bucket
of cinnamon schnapps
back from Kingsgate Mall
& not spill a drop.